the
MISSIONARY'S
LITTLE QUOTE
BOOK

compiled by
R. DALE JEFFERY

Covenant Communications, Inc.

Covenant.

ACTION / MAKING DECISIONS

This is the beginning of a new day. God has given me this day to use as I will. I can waste it—or use it for good, but what I do today is important, because I am exchanging a day of my life for it! When tomorrow comes, this day will be gone forever, leaving in its place something that I have traded for it. I want it to be gain, and not loss; good, and not evil; success, and not failure, in order that I shall not regret the price that I have paid for it.

Dr. Hartsell Wilson

Your faith will perform miracles, especially when you get your hands and feet involved.

Spencer W. Kimball

The past is behind: learn from it.
The future is ahead: prepare for it.
The present is here: live in it!

Thomas S. Monson

All glory comes from daring to begin.

Eugene F. Ware

Indecision mars all success: there can be no good wind for the sailor who knows not to what port he is bound.

Oliver Wendell Holmes

Decision is a sharp knife that cuts clean and straight; indecision is a dull one that hacks and tears and leaves ragged edges behind it.

Anonymous

You seldom get what you go after unless you know in advance what you want. Indecision has often given an advantage to the other fellow because he did his thinking beforehand.

Maurice Switzer

Indecision is fatal. It is better to make the wrong decision than build up a habit of indecision. If you're wallowing in indecision, you certainly can't act—and action is the basis of success.

Marie Beynon Ray

There is no more miserable human than one in whom nothing is habitual but indecision. Full half the time of such a man goes to the deciding, or regretting, of matters which ought to be so ingrained in him as practically not to exist for his consciousness at all.

William James

Ideas bring in nothing unless carried out.

B. C. Forbes

The best answer is to act immediately upon the request.

Anonymous

One today is worth two tomorrows.

Francis Quarles

Today only is thine. If thou procrastinate, thou loseth. Which lost, is lost forever.

Francis Quarles

It is better to be wrong part of the time than to be undecided all of the time.

Anonymous

He who desires much but acts not breeds pestilence.

William Blake

Faith, hope, and charity are ACTIVE principles, not passive ones. If we do not DO them, we don't HAVE them. It's that simple.

Janet Tanner

No man knows what he may accomplish except by trying.

Seneca

It is never too late to be what you might have been.

George Eliot

An idea not coupled with action will become no bigger than the brain cell it occupied.

Arnold H. Glasgow

I am only one, but still I am one; I cannot do everything, but still I can do something; and because I cannot do everything, I will not refuse to do something that I can do.

Edward Everett Hale

Action may not always bring happiness; but there is no happiness without action.

Benjamin Disraeli

To him who is determined it remains only to act.

Italian proverb

A good plan violently executed right now is worth a hundred perfect plans put off until next week.

General George S. Patton

The most drastic and usually the most effective remedy for fear is direct action.

William Burnham

It is better to suffer the worst right now than to live in perpetual fear of it.

Julius Caesar

Our grand business is not to see what lies dimly in the distance, but to *do* what lies clearly at hand.

Thomas Carlyle

There is only one day that you and I have to live for, and that's today. There is nothing we can do about yesterday except repent, and there may be no tomorrow. The thing for us to do when we arise from our beds as God gives us a new day, is to take whatever comes to our hands, and do it to the best of our ability.

Harold B. Lee

Across the plains of time bleach the bones of countless thousands, who, while upon the threshold of victory, sat down to rest. And resting, they died.

Paul H. Dunn

Not what I have but what I DO is my kingdom.

Thomas Carlyle

There is nothing worth more than this day.

Goethe

Perhaps the most valuable result of all education is the ability to make yourself do the thing you have to do when it ought to be done, whether you like it or not. This is the first lesson to be learned.

Thomas Huxley

Life is 10% what happens to us and 90% what we decide to do about it.

Thomas Edison

Decide now that you're not going to be a consumer, or an onlooker, but a *producer*. Decide not to be a sheep, or a hireling, but a *shepherd*.

Richard Stocking

Many people have the right aim in life—but they just never pull the trigger.

Anonymous

This life is the time for men to prepare to meet God; yea, behold the day of this life is the day for men to perform their labors.

Alma 34:32

It is not so much what you believe in that matters, as the way in which you believe it, and proceed to translate that belief into action.

Lin Yutang

Action may not always bring happiness; but there is no happiness without action.

Benjamin Disraeli

A determined soul will do more with a rusty monkey wrench than a loafer will accomplish with all the tools in a machine shop.

Rupert Hughes

Nobody can think straight who does not work. Idleness warps the mind. Thinking without constructive action becomes a disease.

Henry Ford

When a friend is in trouble, don't annoy him by asking if there is anything you can do. Think up something appropriate, and do it.

E. W. Howe

The men who try to do something and fail are infinitely better than those who try to do nothing and succeed.

Lloyd Jones

Life is a piece of paper white
Whereupon each one of us may write
His word or two, and then comes night.

Greatly begin! Though thou have time
But for a line, be that sublime—
Not failure,
        but low aim
                is crime.

Percival Lowell

But be ye doers of the word, and not hearers only,
deceiving your own selves.

James 1:22

If you ever need a helping hand, look at the end
of your arm.

Bryan B. Gardner

A kindness put off until tomorrow becomes only a bitter regret.

Anonymous

What would be the use of eternity to a person who cannot use well one half hour ?

Emerson

Today is the only time we can possibly live.

Dale Carnegie

Procrastination is the thief of time.

Edward Young

Worse than a quitter is the one who is afraid to begin.

Anonymous

"Don't waste your time collecting other people's autographs," George Bernard Shaw once wrote to a young lad who pushed a pencil in his hand. "Rather, devote it to making your own autograph worth collecting."

There are three kinds of people in this world: there are those who watch things happen and those who make things happen. And then there are the people who wonder what happened!

Anonymous

It is accounted unto you for righteousness if you proceed according to the best light you have.

Wilford Woodruff

Begin: to have begun is half the work. Let the half still remain; again begin this and thou wilt have done all.

Ausonius

Destiny is not a matter of chance, but of *choice*; it is not a thing to be waited for, but a thing to be *achieved*.

William Jennings Bryan

To do today's work well and not bother about tomorrow is the secret of accomplishment.

William Osler

Perhaps the most valuable result of all education is the ability to make yourself do the thing you have to do when it ought to be done, whether you like it or not. This is the first lesson to be learned.

Thomas Huxley

I have generally found that a man who is good at an excuse is good at nothing else.

Benjamin Franklin

People with reasons for their actions seldom need excuses.

Anonymous

Attitude / Perspective

Said one bucket to the other: "Whenever I get filled up, I get emptied out real soon."
Said the other bucket: "Whenever I get emptied out, I am ready to be filled again."

Anonymous

I have learned from experience that the greater part of our happiness or misery depends on our dispositions and not on our circumstances.

Martha Washington

They are never alone who are accompanied with noble thoughts.

Philip Sydney

"I cannot" never accomplished anything. "I will try" has wrought wonders.

Joel Hawes

I do the very best I know how; the very best I can; and I mean to keep doing so until the end.
 If the end brings me out all right, what is said against me won't amount to anything.

Abraham Lincoln

Verily I say unto you, Except ye be converted, and become as little children, ye shall not enter into the kingdom of heaven.

Matthew 18:3

There is always a frontier where there is an open mind and a willing hand.

Charles F. Kettering

He who knows others is clever, but he who knows himself is enlightened.

Lao Tse

You have powers you never dreamed of. You can do things you never thought you could do. There are no limitations in what you can do except the limitations as to what you cannot do. Don't think you cannot. Think that you can.

Darwin P. Kingsley

If you cannot win yourself, then make the one ahead of you break the record.

Anonymous

The secret of happiness is to count your blessings while others are adding up their troubles.

Anonymous

You can often gauge a man's ambition by whether he hates his alarm clock or considers it his best friend.

Thomas Edison

Never despair, but if you do, work on in despair.

Edmund Burke

Anybody who has the mind to do it can. So it's having the mind for it that counts.

Jacob M. Braude

It is amazing what ordinary people can do if they set out without preconceived notions.

Charles F. Kettering

Reflect on your present blessings, of which every man has many; not on your past misfortunes, of which all men have some.

Charles Dickens

Out of the lowest depths there is the path to the highest heights.

Thomas Carlyle

There is only one thing more contagious than enthusiasm, and that is the lack of enthusiasm.

Thomas S. Monson

Nothing great was ever achieved without enthusiasm.

Emerson

Years may wrinkle the skin, but the lack of enthusiasm will wrinkle the soul.

Anonymous

To enter heaven a man must take it with him.

Henry Drummond

- Embrace the quest for excellence.
- Nobody is above the basics.
- Your attitude can be a "positude" or a
  "negatude." Choose the positude.
- This is my best day so far.

Cecilia Peachey

It's your **attitude**, not your **aptitude**, which deter-
mines your **altitude** in life.

Dave Dean

We see things not as they are, but as WE are.

H. M. Tomlinson

The only people you should try to get even with are the ones who've helped you out.

Anonymous

You can either complain that the roses have thorns, or thank God that the thorns have roses!

Anonymous

We are not human beings having a spiritual experience: we are spiritual beings having a human experience.

Tielhard de Chardin

Nice guys only *appear* to finish last—actually, they are running a different race.

Anonymous

What lies behind us and what lies before us are tiny matters compared to what lies within us.

Ralph Waldo Emerson

The greatest discovery of my age is that men can change their circumstances by changing the attitude of their minds.

William James

When an optimist finds a worm in an apple, he goes fishing.

Anonymous

To most people, seeing is believing. To the select few, however, *believing is seeing*.

Anonymous

We make our own destiny. . . . We can satisfy ourselves with mediocrity. We can be common, ordinary, dull, colorless, or we can so channel our lives to be clean, vibrant, progressive, colorful, and rich.

Spencer W. Kimball

Life isn't fair, but we can still expect the best from ourselves.

*E. St. Louis Coach, quoted by
Marvin J. Ashton*

Life is full of people who will tell you what you can't ever achieve. Successful people hang around those who tell them what they *can* achieve.

R. Dale Jeffery

AVOIDING TEMPTATION AND CONTENTION

No one ever fell over a precipice who never went near one.

Richard L. Evans

It is one thing to be tempted,
And another thing to fall.

William Shakespeare

Watch and pray, that ye enter not into temptation: the spirit indeed is willing, but the flesh is weak.

Matthew 26:41

Prove all things; hold fast that which is good. Abstain from all appearance of evil.

1 Thessalonians 5:21-22

"Do not forget," said the Devil with a smile, "that I have been evolving, too."

Dean William Ralph Infe

If you don't want temptation to follow you, don't act as if you are interested.

Richard L. Evans

The only safe ground is to get as far from danger as it is possible to get.

Heber J. Grant

The nearer a person approaches the Lord, the greater power will be manifest by the Adversary to prevent the accomplishment of his purpose.

Heber C. Kimball

Temptations and worries are a bit like the birds of the air. You can't prevent them from flying around your head, but you can keep them from making a nest in your hair.

Martin Luther

Cease to contend one with another; cease to speak evil one of another.

Doctrine & Covenants 136:23

Reckon the days in which you have not been angry. I used to be angry every day; now every other day; then every third and fourth day; and if you miss it as long as thirty days, offer a sacrifice of thanksgiving to God.

Epictetus

So long as a man is angry he cannot be right.

Chinese proverb

Anger is never without a reason, but seldom with a good one.

Benjamin Franklin

When angry, count to ten before you speak; if you're very angry, count to a hundred.

Thomas Jefferson

When anger rises, think of the consequences.

Confucius

I do not fight with my many detractors. I criticize not by finding fault but with a new creation.

Michelangelo

Neither irony or sarcasm is [a good] argument.

Joseph H. Choate

Obstinacy and vehemency in opinion are the surest proof of stupidity.

Bernard Barton

Too many opinions which are expressed should have gone by slow freight.

Francis O. Walsh

A truth that's told with bad intent
Beats all the lies you can invent.

William Blake

To ignore an insult is the true test of courage.

Anonymous

Derision is the argument of a fool.

*Cardinal Francesco da
Quignonez*

A soft answer turneth away wrath: but grievous
words stir up anger.

Proverbs 15:1

The best answer to anger is silence.

German proverb

Trying to settle an argument with harsh words is
like trying to unsnarl traffic by blowing horns.

Anonymous

You cannot *antagonize* and *influence* at the same time.

J. S. Knox

He that is slow to anger is better than the mighty; and he that ruleth his spirit than he that taketh a city.

Proverbs 16:32

Building Relationships of Trust / Conversation and Listening Skills

You can make more friends in two months by becoming interested in other people than you can in two years by trying to get other people interested in you.

Dale Carnegie

Strangers are just friends you haven't met yet. I never met a man I didn't like.

Will Rogers

For good or ill, your conversation is your advertisement. For every time you open your mouth, you let men look into your mind. Do they see it neat and well—clothed and businesslike?

Bruce Barton

The time to stop talking is when the other person nods his head affirmatively but says nothing.

Henry S. Haskins

The best way to win an argument is to avoid it.

Anonymous

A good listener is not only popular everywhere, but after a while he knows something.

Wilson Mizner

The art of being wise is the ability to know what to overlook.

William James

If you can't find something good in your vocabulary to say about a person, smile.

Anonymous

You can either impress people with the quality of what you say, or kill them with the quantity.

J. Brockman Lenox

Before you speak, know your audience.

Anonymous

EXAMPLE

Be thou an example of the believers, in word, in conversation, in charity, in spirit, in faith, in purity.

1 Timothy 4:12

A good example is the best sermon.

Anonymous

Let your light so shine before men, that they may see your good works, and glorify your Father which is in Heaven.

Matthew 5:16

Therefore let your light so shine before this people, that they may see your good works, and glorify your Father who is in heaven.

3 Nephi 12:16

We cannot make others do the right things. We can only show them by our example what "doing the right things" looks like.

Kay Stevens

He who lives well is the best preacher.

Miguel de Cervantes

Read Alma Chapter 4: Wickedness and pride within the church becomes a stumbling block to its progress, because of the poor example that some members set.

People pay very little attention to what you say about your religion—they're too busy watching what you do about it.

Anonymous

He that gives good advice builds with one hand; he that gives good counsel and example builds with both; but he that gives good admonition and bad example builds with one hand and pulls down with the other.

Francis Bacon

He must often change who would be constant in happiness or wisdom.

Confucius

There are three ways to teach: by example, example, and example.

Anonymous

We carry upon our shoulders the reputation of the Church—each and every one of us.

Heber J. Grant

Verily I say unto you all: Arise and shine forth, that thy light may be a standard for the nations.

Doctrine & Covenants 115:5

FREE AGENCY / CHOICES

For behold, ye are free; ye are permitted to act for yourselves; for behold, God hath given unto you a knowledge and he hath made you free. He hath given unto you that ye might know good from evil, and he hath given you that ye might choose life or death; and ye can do good and be restored unto that which is good, . . . or ye can do evil, and have that which is evil restored unto you.

Helaman 14:30-31

Therefore, cheer up your hearts, and remember that ye are free to act for yourselves——to choose the way of everlasting death or the way of eternal life.

2 Nephi 10:23

Life is the acceptance of responsibilities, or their evasion. It is the business of meeting obligations or avoiding them. To every man the choice is continually being offered, and by the manner of his choosing you may fairly measure him.

Ben Amos Williams

Do what is right, let the consequence follow
Battle for freedom in spirit and might
And with stout hearts look ye forth till tomorrow;
God will protect you; do what is right!

LDS Hymns, No. 237

Your destiny is in your hands, and your important decisions are your own to make.

Spencer W. Kimball

When faced with a crisis, the man of character falls back on himself. He imposes his own stamp on action, takes responsibility for it, and makes it his own.

Charles DeGaulle

It makes a difference to all eternity, whether we do right or wrong today.

James F. Clark

Therefore repent ye, repent ye, lest by knowing these things and not doing them ye shall suffer yourselves to come under condemnation.

Helaman 14:19

For what is the most choiceworthy for each individual is the highest it is possible for him to achieve.

Aristotle

For behold, it is not meet that I should command in all things; for he that is compelled in all things, the same is a slothful and not a wise servant; wherefore he receiveth no reward.

Doctrine & Covenants 58:26

Wherefore, men are free according to the flesh; and all things are given them which are expedient unto man. And they are free to choose liberty and eternal life, through the great Mediator of all men, or to choose captivity and death, according to the captivity and power of the devil; for he seeketh that all men might be miserable like unto himself.

2 Nephi 2:27

THE HOLY SPIRIT

I will impart unto you of my Spirit, which shall enlighten your mind, which shall fill your soul with joy;
And then shall ye know, or by this shall you know, all things whatsoever you desire of me.

Doctrine & Covenants
11:13-14

Work smarter. Believe more. Listen for the promptings of the Holy Spirit. Trust your own judgment.

Gordon B. Hinckley

For the Spirit of the Lord will not always strive with man. And when the Spirit ceaseth to strive with man then cometh speedy destruction.

2 Nephi 26:11

"I want you to teach the people—and I want you to follow this counsel yourself—that they must labor and so live as to obtain the Holy Spirit, for without this you cannot build up the kingdom; without the spirit of God you are in danger of walking in the dark, and in danger of failing to accomplish your calling as apostles and as elders in the church and kingdom of God."

Brigham Young to
Wilford Woodruff

Ten Gifts of The Holy Spirit:

1. Helps us understand what we see and hear.

2. Helps us to recognize the truth.

3. Helps us make decisions.

4. Helps us to know and choose the right.

5. Inspires us with thoughts and ideas.

6. Helps us to understand and communicate with each other.

7. Helps us recall important things when we need them.

8. Warns us of danger.

9. Comforts us when we stand in need of comfort.

10. Helps us build a testimony for ourselves of the truth.

Henry B. Eyring

When a man speaketh by the power of the Holy Ghost the power of the Holy Ghost carrieth it unto the hearts of the children of men.

2 Nephi 33:1

But the fruit of the Spirit is love, joy, peace, long-suffering, gentleness, goodness, faith, meekness, temperance.

Galatians 5:22-23

I have come to know that the witness of the Spirit does not come by seeking after signs. It comes through fasting and prayer, through activity and testing and obedience. It comes through sustaining the servants of the Lord and following them.

Boyd K. Packer

And it came to pass when they heard this voice, and beheld that it was not a voice of thunder, neither was it a voice of a great tumultuous noise, but behold, it was a still voice of perfect mildness, as if it had been a whisper, and it did pierce even to the very soul.

Helaman 5:30

The only tyrant I accept is the "still small voice" within.

Mahatma Gandhi

To be forever reaching out, to remain unsatisfied, is the key to spiritual progress.

Arden Engebretsen

And now, verily, verily, I say unto thee, put your trust in that Spirit which leadeth to do good— yea, to do justly, to walk humbly, to judge righteously; and this is my Spirit.

Verily, verily, I say unto you, I will impart unto you of my Spirit, which shall enlighten your mind, which shall fill your soul with joy;

And then shall ye know, or by this shall ye know, all things whatsoever you desire of me, which are pertaining unto things of righteousness, in faith believing in me that you shall receive.

Doctrine & Covenants
11:12-14, italics added

HARD WORK

It is for us to make the effort. The result is always in God's hands.

Mahatma Gandhi

Let us realize that the privilege to work is a gift, the power to work is a blessing, the love of work is success. Genius undoubtedly is little more than the capacity for hard, sustained work.

David O. McKay

Work while you have the light. You are responsible for the talent that has been entrusted to you.

Henri F. Amiel

My suggestion to ambitious young men would be to conserve and develop their physical and mental strength, cram their heads with all the useful knowledge they can, and work, work, work—not simply for their own advancement but to get worthwhile things done.

Edward G. Seubert

If you ever need a helping hand, look at the end of your arm.

Bryan B. Gardner

Pray as if everything depended on God and then work as if everything depended on you.

Francis Cardinal Spellman

It is praiseworthy even to attempt a great action.

*François de la
Rouchefoucald*

Diligence is the mother of good fortune, and God gives abundantly to industry. So plow deep while the sluggards sleep, and you shall have corn to sell and to keep.

Benjamin Franklin

If you have great talents, industriousness will improve them; if you have but moderate abilities, industry will supply their deficiencies.

Samuel Smiles

Be faithful and diligent in keeping the commandments of God, and I will encircle thee in the arms of my love.

Doctrine & Covenants 6:20

Ask, and it shall be given unto you; seek, and ye shall find; knock, and it shall be opened unto you.

3 Nephi 14:7

Even so faith, if it hath not works, is dead, being alone.

James 2:17

Therefore, O ye that embark in the service of God, see that ye serve him with all your heart, might, mind and strength, that ye may stand blameless before God at the last day.

Doctrine & Covenants 4:2

But be ye doers of the word, and not hearers only, deceiving your own selves.

James 1:22

He who lives well is the best preacher.

Miguel de Cervantes

Wherefore, be not weary in well-doing, for ye are laying the foundation of a great work. And out of small things proceedeth that which is great.

Doctrine & Covenants 64:33

Our only concern should be to do better than we did yesterday. Step by step is the law of growth. God does not expect the acorn to be a mighty oak before it has been a sapling.

George E. Carpenter

Hard workers are usually honest; industry lifts them above temptation.

Christian Neville Bovee

If the power to do hard work is not talent, it is the best possible substitute for it.

James A. Garfield

I am wondering what would have happened to me if some fluent talker had converted me to the theory of the eight-hour day and convinced me that it was not fair to my fellow workers to put forth my best efforts in my work. . . . If my life had been made up of eight-hour days I do not believe I could have accomplished a great deal.

Thomas A. Edison

Do the duty which lies nearest thee. Thy second duty will already have become clearer.

Thomas Carlyle

Wherefore, now let every man learn his duty, and to act in the office in which he is appointed, in all diligence.

Doctrine & Covenants 107:99

Make it a point to do something every day that you don't want to do. This is the golden rule for acquiring the habit of doing your duty without pain.

Mark Twain

Do your duty, and leave the rest to Heaven.

Pierre Corneille

Work is the true elixir of life. The busiest man is the happiest man. Excellence in any art or profession is attained only by hard and persistent work. Never believe that you are perfect. When a man imagines, even after years of striving, that he has attained perfection, his decline begins.

Sir Theodore Martin

The trouble with an opportunity is that it always comes disguised as hard work.

Will Rogers

We rate ability in men by what they finish, not by what they attempt.

N. MacDonald

For anything worth having one must pay the price; and the price is always work, patience, love, self-sacrifice—no paper currency, no promises to pay, but the gold of real service.

John Burroughs

It's great to have your feet on the ground—but keep them moving. Nobody can think straight who does not work. Idleness warps the mind. Thinking without constructive action becomes a disease.

Henry Ford

One of the most durable satisfactions in life is to lose one's self in one's work.

Henry Emerson Fosdick

The joy of living comes from immersion in something that we know to be bigger, better, more enduring and worthier than we are.

John Mason Brown

It is only those who do not know how to work that do not love it. To those who do, it is better than play.

J. H. Patterson

Do your work well—God's recompense to you is the power to do greater things.

Quoted by Lucy Gertsch Thomson

Don't be fooled by the calendar. There are only as many days in the year as you make use of. One man gets only a week's value out of a year, while another gets a full year's value out of a week.

Charles Richards

The highest possible reward for any man's toil is not what he gets for it, but what he becomes by it.

John Ruskin

Life is not what you want it to be, but what you make it. Your ship *has* come in. . . but you've got to row out to meet it.

Anonymous

Unless a man undertakes more than he can possibly do, he will never do all that he can.

Henry Ford

Work will win when wishy-washy wishing won't.

The "W" formula, from
Thomas S. Monson

Edison once was asked how he accomplished so much. He said, "It is deceptively simple. You and I have eighteen hours in a day in which we do something. You spend that eighteen hours doing a number of unrelated things. I spend it doing just one thing, and some of my work is bound to amount to something."

Sterling W. Sill

God gives every bird his food, but He does not throw it in its nest.

J. G. Holland

To do today's work well and not bother about tomorrow is the secret of accomplishment.

William Osler

You learn to do by doing. You learn to be by being.

H. Burke Peterson

Did you ever hear of a man who had striven all his life faithfully and singly toward an object, and in no measure obtained it? If a man constantly aspires, is he not elevated? Did ever a man try heroism, magnanimity, truth, sincerity, and find that there was no advantage in them—that it was a vain endeavor?

Henry David Thoreau

The main satisfactions in life come through hard work which one enjoys.

Charles W. Eliot

He who rolls up his sleeves seldom loses his shirt.

Anonymous

Fear not to do good, my sons, for whatsoever ye sow, that shall ye also reap; therefore, if ye sow good ye shall also reap good for your reward.

Doctrine & Covenants 6:33

Commit thy works unto the Lord, and thy thoughts shall be established.

Proverbs 16:3

If you make your job important, it's quite likely to return the favor.

Anonymous

Jesus Christ / Discipleship

We talk of Christ, we rejoice in Christ, we preach of Christ, we prophesy of Christ, and we write according to our prophecies, that our children may know to what source they may look for a remission of their sins.

2 Nephi 25:26

Jesus will save you
  Just as you are;
Jesus will welcome you
  back from afar;
Jesus will heal
  sin's pitiful scar:
Just as you are,
  come home.

John Runyon

Come unto me, all ye that labour and are heavy laden, and I will give you rest.

Matthew 11:28

Yea, remember that there is no other way nor means whereby man can be saved, only through the atoning blood of Jesus Christ.

Helaman 5:9

And he gave some, apostles; and some, prophets; and some, evangelists; and some, pastors and teachers;
For the perfecting of the saints, for the work of the ministry, for the edifying of the body of Christ.

Ephesians 4:11-12

Yea, thus we see that the gate of heaven is open unto all, even to those who will believe on the name of Jesus Christ, who is the Son of God.

Helaman 3:28

And this is life eternal, that they might know thee the only true God, and Jesus Christ, whom thou hast sent.

John 17:3

Behold, Jesus Christ is the name which is given of the Father, and there is none other name given whereby man can be saved;
Wherefore, all men must take upon them the name which is given of the Father, for in that name shall they be called at the last day.

Doctrine & Covenants
18:23-24

For where two or three are gathered together in my name, there am I in the midst of them.

Matthew 18:20

The Lord is my shepherd; I shall not want.
He maketh me to lie down in green pastures: he leadeth me beside the still waters.
He restoreth my soul: he leadeth me in the paths of righteousness for his name's sake.
Yea, though I walk through the valley of the shadow of death, I will fear no evil: for thou art with me; thy rod and thy staff they comfort me.
Thou preparest a table before me in the presence of mine enemies: thou anointest my head with oil; my cup runneth over.
Surely goodness and mercy shall follow me all the days of my life: and I will dwell in the house of the Lord for ever.

Psalms 23

Seek ye the Lord while he may be found, call ye upon him while he is near.

Isaiah 55:6

From that time many of his disciples went back, and walked no more with him.
Then said Jesus unto the twelve, Will ye also go away?
Then Simon Peter answered him, Lord, to whom shall we go? thou hast the words of eternal life.
And we believe and are sure that thou art that Christ, the Son of the living God.

John 6: 66-69

My sheep hear my voice, and I know them, and they follow me.

John 10:27

Behold, I am Jesus Christ, whom the prophets testified shall come into the world. . . . I am the light and the life of the world. . . . Whoso believeth in me, and is baptized, the same shall be saved; and they are they who shall inherit the kingdom of God.

3 Nephi 11:10-11, 33

Wherefore, be of good cheer, and do not fear, for I the Lord am with you, and will stand by you; and ye shall bear record of me, even Jesus Christ, that I am the Son of the living God, that I was, that I am, and that I am to come.

Doctrine & Covenants 68:6

And this is the gospel, the glad tidings, which the voice out of the heavens bore record unto us—
That he came into the world, even Jesus, to be crucified for the world, and to bear the sins of the world, and to sanctify the world, and to cleanse it from all unrighteousness;
That through him all might be saved whom the Father had put into his power and made by him.

Doctrine & Covenants
76:40-42

If you want your neighbor to see what Christ's spirit will do for him, let him see what it has done for you.

Henry Ward Beecher

Beloved, now we are the sons of God . . . we know that, when he shall appear, we shall be like him; for we shall see him as he is.

1 John 3:2

And now, my sons, remember, remember that it is upon the rock of our Redeemer, who is Christ, the Son of God, that ye must build your foundation; that when the devil shall send forth his mighty winds, yea, his shafts in the whirlwind, yea, when all his hail and his mighty storm shall beat upon you, it shall have no power over you to drag you down to the gulf of misery and endless wo, because of the rock upon which ye are built, which is a sure foundation, a foundation whereon if men build they cannot fall.

Helaman 5:12

And now, after the many testimonies which have been given of him, this is the testimony, last of all, which we give of him: That he lives!

For we saw him, even on the right hand of God; and we heard the voice bearing record that he is the Only Begotten of the Father—

That by him, and through him, and of him, the worlds are and were created, and the inhabitants thereof are begotten sons and daughters unto God.

Doctrine & Covenants
76:22-24

LOVE / CHARITY

God is love; and he that dwelleth in love dwelleth in God, and God in him.

1 John 4:16

And thou shalt love the Lord thy God with all thine heart, and with all thy soul, and with all thy might.

Deuteronomy 6:5

Give, and it shall be given unto you. . . . For with the same measure that ye mete withal it shall be measured to you again.

Luke 6:38

But I say unto you, Love your enemies, bless them that curse you, do good to them that hate you, and pray for them which despitefully use you, and persecute you.

Matthew 5:44

When a friend is in trouble, don't annoy him by asking if there is anything you can do. Think up something appropriate, and do it.

E. W. Howe

And the Lord called his people Zion, because they were of one heart and one mind, and dwelt in righteousness; and there was no poor among them.

Moses 7:18

But charity is the pure love of Christ, and it endureth forever; and whoso is found possessed of it at the last day, it shall be well with him.

Moroni 7:47

Charity fixes no blame: she sees the need, not the cause.

German proverb

A kindness put off until tomorrow becomes only a bitter regret.

Anonymous

Six of the greatest words on earth:

> Control Thyself—*Cicero*
> Know Thyself—*Socrates*
> Give Thyself—*Christ*

A good deed is never lost; he who sows courtesy reaps friendship, and he who plants kindness gathers love.

St. Basil

The deepest principle of human nature is the craving to be appreciated.

William James

Heaven is the consciousness of having made the world a better place to live in.

Elaine L. Jack

Giving is true having.

Charles H. Spurgeon

In this world, it is not what we take up but what we give up that makes us rich.

Henry Ward Beecher

Are you one of those in the "I hate to" family? How often one hears people use that phrase. If you are guilty of using it, try to break yourself of the habit. It doesn't reflect a strong, healthy, vigorous mental attitude. It suggests pettiness, querulousness, and lack of the "I will" spirit. The way to conquer a disposition to "hate" so many things is to cultivate a cheerful, resolute, beneficial frame of mind. If you fill your heart with love of your fellow-mortals and are possessed of a consuming desire to be of service in the world, you will have little room left in you for "hating" this, that, and the next thing or person. The forceful person, animated by the right motives, starts more sentences with the words "I like to" than "I hate to." Get this thought into your mind. If you are constantly "hating," the cause lies within yourself.

B.C. Forbes

Kindness is a treasure, but practice is the key to it.

Anonymous

Kindness means doing a lot of little things kindly and always, not just a big thing now and then.

Neville Hobson

I cannot do great things by myself, but I can do small things in a great way.

James Freeman Clarke

He that findeth his life shall lose it: and he that loseth his life for my sake shall find it.

Matthew 10:39

I have wept in the night
for the shortness of sight
That to somebody's need made me blind;
But I never have yet
Felt a twinge of regret
For being a little too kind.

Unknown

Kindness is a language which the deaf can hear
and the blind can read.

Mark Twain

To ease another's heartache is to forget one's own.

Abraham Lincoln

Only a life lived for others is a life worthwhile.

Albert Einstein

A stingy man is always poor.

French proverb

For anything worth having one must pay the price; and the price is always work, patience, love, self-sacrifice—no paper currency, no promises to pay, but the gold of real service.

John Burroughs

God does notice us, and He watches over us. But it is usually through another person that He meets our needs.

Spencer W. Kimball

Charity is the ability to separate the man from the things he does.

Hyrum Smith

This is the true test of love—to respect and serve those who can be of no use to us at all.

Anonymous

The only people you should try to get even with are those who've helped you out.

Anonymous

When sowing seeds
Of friendly deeds,
The less you keep
The more you reap.

Christopher Bannister

The noblest service comes from nameless hands,
and the best servant does his work unseen.

Anonymous

What a great difference there is between giving
advice and lending a hand!

Anonymous

Charity is the greatest gift of all, and without it all else will fail. If we had any idea what is really in store for us, we would not waste time on the undesirable.

Chauncey C. Riddle

He who scatters has much: he who takes for himself has little.

Lao Tse

Let your love be unconditional—you only fail when you fail to try.

Spencer W. Kimball

Love does not die easily—it is a living thing. It thrives in the face of all life's hazards save one: neglect.

Anonymous

A candle that lights another loses no light itself.

Anonymous

Love one human being purely and warmly, and you will love all.

Johann Richter

The three hardest tasks in the world are neither physical feats nor intellectual achievements, but moral acts: to return love for hate, to include the excluded, and to say, "I was wrong."

Sydney J. Harris

Escape from the prison of yourself, and you have stepped into a wonderful new world.

Robert O. Cummins

There are two kinds of people in the world; those you love and those you don't know yet.

Anonymous

A good deed is never lost; he who sows courtesy reaps friendship, and he who plants kindness gathers love.

St. Basil

Where there is hatred, let me sow love. Where there is injury, pardon. Where there is doubt, faith. Where there is despair, hope. Where there is darkness, light. Where there is sadness, joy. O Divine Master, grant that I may not so much seek to be consoled as to console; to be understood, as to understand; to be loved, as to love; for it is in giving that we receive; it is in pardoning that we are pardoned, and it is in dying that we are born to Eternal Life.

St. Francis of Assisi

There's a destiny that makes us brothers,
None goes his way alone.
All that we send into the lives of others
Will come back into our own.

Edwin Markham

Life is not so short but there is always time for courtesy.

Thomas S. Monson

LEADERSHIP

A nd when thou art converted, strengthen thy brethren.

Luke 22:32

Let your light so shine before men, that they may see your good works, and glorify your Father which is in Heaven.

Matthew 5:16

Therefore, strengthen your brethren in all your conversation, in all your prayers, in all your exhortations, and in all your doings.

Doctrine & Covenants 108:7

Once in a while a man is born who is not afraid. Then things begin to move. "I must do something" will solve more problems than "something must be done."

Bruce Barton

The meaning of history is never apparent to those who make it; a leader in any age or generation is no more than a man who sees somewhat beyond the end of his nose.

Thomas Sugrue

Little progress can be made by merely attempting to repress what is evil; our great hope lies in developing what is good.

Calvin Coolidge

Coming together is a beginning;
Keeping together is progress.
Working together is success.

Anonymous

My grandmother told us that there would be many
and great obstacles in our paths and that this was
the way of life. But only weaklings give up in the
face of obstacles. . . . Be honest and frank with
yourself and the world at all times. Never compro-
mise what you know to be right. Never pick a
fight, but never run from one when your principles are at stake. . . . Go out into the world with
your head high and keep it high at all times.

Ralph J. Bunche

Technical training is important, but it accounts for less than 20% of one's success. More than 80% is due to the development of one's personal qualities, such as initiative, thoroughness, concentration, decision, adaptability, organizing ability, observation, industry and leadership.

Dr. G. P. Koch

Good management consists in showing average people how to do the work of superior people.

John D. Rockefeller

Real leaders are ordinary people with extraordinary determinations.

John Seaman Garns

The man who commands efficiently must have obeyed others in the past.

Cicero

A great leader never sets himself above his followers, except in carrying responsibilities.

Anonymous

A good leader takes a little more than his share of blame; a little less than his share of credit.

Arnold H. Glasgow

Education is the mother of leadership.

Wendell Wilkie

Few people are born leaders. Leadership is achieved by ability, alertness, experience and keeping posted; by willingness to accept responsibility; a knack of getting along with people; an open mind; and a head that stays clear under stress.

Franklin Field

Business history is full of men who never were class officers or team captains but became important leaders. Occasionally, leaders are "born." Often leaders are "made." But more often they are "self-made."

Anonymous

If you are not afraid to face the music, you may get to lead the band some day.

Edwin H. Stuart

The new leadership is clearly distinguished from the old-style boss. A boss creates fear—a leader confidence; a boss fixes blame—a leader corrects mistakes; a boss knows it all—a leader asks questions; a boss makes work drudgery—a leader makes it interesting and challenging; a boss is interested in himself—a leader, in the group.

Russell H. Ewing

Mediocrity always associates with those who aren't impatient with it.

François de la Rouchefoucald

Great men think of opportunity, not time. Time is the excuse of feeble and puzzled spirits.

Benjamin Disraeli

Good management is not only the gift of identifying talent, but the art of selective recognition of strength and weakness, and the proper encouragement of the best in any man or woman.

Anonymous

The most important position in the Church is the one you presently hold.

Antoine R. Ivins

Remember—no matter what field you are in, a person can never be greater as a leader than he is as an individual.

Anonymous

Bless us with a desire to reach thy kingdom, and to bring those we love with us.

Rusty Clark

Never discourage anyone who continually makes progress, no matter how slow.

Plato

The least of us, the humblest, is in partnership with the Almighty to bring to pass the salvation of the human family. We are all to be Saviors of Mt. Zion.

John A. Widtsoe

The man who follows the crowd will never be followed by the crowd.

Anonymous

Where e'er thou art, act well thy part.

David O. McKay

It isn't enough to do one's best. One must do what is necessary.

Winston Churchill

You cannot teach a man anything. You can only help him to find it within himself.

Galileo

Not everybody can lead the group at once. One person typically gets called, and they hold the title of "leader." But there are two distinct types of leadership:

LEADERSHIP I
- Take Charge
- Provide Equity for Everyone
- Accomplish the Mission
- Make Decisions and Solve Problems as Necessary
- Follow Through With Commitments

LEADERSHIP II
- Second the Leader's Opinion
- Follow Through With Delegated Duties
- Help the Leader Make Proper Decisions
- Provide Good Ideas and Feedback
- Encourage Harmony and Teamwork within the group as necessary

Ricardo Diaz

A big man shows his bigness by the way he treats little people.

Anonymous

The buck stops here.

Harry S. Truman

One person working with you is worth a dozen working for you.

Anonymous

Paddle your own canoe, even if your dad owns a ship.

Quoted by James M. Braude

He who wishes to secure the good of others has already secured his own.

Confucius

You will never have a greater or lesser dominion than that over yourself. The height of a man's success is gauged by his self-mastery; the depths of his failure by his self-abandonment. He who cannot establish dominion over himself will have no dominion over others.

Leonardo da Vinci

The people who get on in this world are the people who get up and look for the circumstances they want; if they don't find them, they *make* them.

George Bernard Shaw

Little progress can be made by merely attempting to repress what is evil; our great hope lies in developing what is good.

Calvin Coolidge

It matters not how straight the gate,
How charged with punishments the scroll.
I am the master of my fate:
I am the captain of my soul.

William E. Henley

It is not the critic who counts; not the one who points out how the strong man stumbled or how the doer of great deeds might have done better. The credit belongs to the man who is actually in the arena, whose face is marred by sweat and dust and blood; who strives valiantly; who errs and comes up short again and again; who knows the great enthusiasms, the great devotions, and spends himself in a worthy cause; who if he wins knows the triumph of great achievement; and who, if he fails, at least fails while daring greatly, so that his place shall never be with those cold and timid souls who know neither victory nor defeat.

Theodore Roosevelt, quoted by
John F. Kennedy in his
Inaugural Address

It is a thing of no great difficulty to raise objections against a man's oration—nay, it is a very easy matter; but to produce a better in its place is a work extremely troublesome.

Plutarch

That which gets recognized and reinforced gets done. That which doesn't get recognized and reinforced doesn't get done.

*"The Greatest Management
Principle in the World"*

Do not go where the path may lead. Go instead where there is no path, and blaze a trail.

Anonymous

Working - Doing the job the required way for the required number of hours.

Efficiency - Doing the required job well.

Effectiveness - Doing the RIGHT job, and doing it well.

Creative Muscle - Actively applying creativity and hard work to find new solutions to ongoing problems and situations.

Leadership - Figuring out what is the next thing that should be done, and getting on with it. (Read Alma 18:8-10.)

R. Dale Jeffery

MISSIONARY WORK

L ift up your heart and rejoice, for the hour of your mission is come.

Doctrine & Covenants 31:3

Say nothing but repentance unto this generation; keep my commandments, and assist to bring forth my work, according to my commandments, and you shall be blessed.

Doctrine & Covenants 6:9

Ye are called to bring to pass the gathering of my elect; for mine elect hear my voice and harden not their hearts.

Doctrine & Covenants 29:7

Now behold, a marvelous work is about to come forth among the children of men.

Therefore, O ye that embark in the service of God, see that ye serve him with all your heart, might, mind and strength, that ye may stand blameless before God at the last day.

Therefore, if ye have desires to serve God ye are called to the work;

For behold the field is white already to harvest; and lo, he that thrusteth in his sickle with his might, the same layeth up in store that he perisheth not, but bringeth salvation to his soul;

And faith, hope, charity and love, with an eye single to the glory of God, qualify him for the work.

Remember faith, virtue, knowledge, temperance, patience, brotherly kindness, godliness, charity, humility, diligence.

Ask, and ye shall receive; knock, and it shall be opened unto you. Amen.

Doctrine & Covenants
Section 4

Thou shalt declare repentance and faith on the Savior, and remission of sins by baptism, and by fire, yea, even the Holy Ghost.

Behold, this is a great and the last commandment which I shall give unto you concerning this matter; for this shall suffice for thy daily walk, even unto the end of thy life.

Doctrine & Covenants
19:31-32

Let's work! I shall go to my grave saying that missionaries generally speaking never rise in their entire life above the stature they carve out for themselves in the mission field.

Henry D. Moyle

The first great commandment is to love the Lord our God with all our hearts, might, mind and strength: and the second is like unto it, to love our neighbors as ourselves. And the best way in the world to show our love for our neighbor is to go forth and proclaim the gospel of the Lord Jesus Christ, of which he has given us an absolute knowledge concerning its divinity.

Heber J. Grant

Where two or three are gathered together in my name . . . there will I be in the midst of them.

Doctrine & Covenants 6:32

Behold, the field is white already to harvest; therefore, whoso desireth to reap, let him thrust in his sickle with his might, and reap while the day lasts, that he may treasure up for his soul everlasting salvation in the kingdom of God.

Doctrine & Covenants 6:3

The thing which will be of the most worth unto you will be to declare repentance unto this people, that you may bring souls unto me, that you may rest with them in the kingdom of my Father.

Doctrine & Covenants 15:6

You are called upon to declare the words of eternal life with vigor, humility and faith— bringing out of darkness those that sit in darkness.

Joseph Fielding Smith

After all that has been said, the greatest and most important duty is to preach the gospel.

Joseph Smith, Jr.

Seek not to declare my word, but first seek to obtain my word, and then shall your tongue be loosed; then, if you desire, you shall have my Spirit and my word, yea, the power of God unto the convincing of men.

Doctrine & Covenants 11:21

And we did magnify our office unto the Lord, taking upon us the responsibility, answering the sins of the people upon our own heads if we did not teach them the word of God with all diligence; wherefore, by laboring with our might their blood might not come upon our garments; . . . and we would not be found spotless at the last day.

Jacob 1:19

Go in all meekness and sobriety, and preach Jesus Christ and Him crucified; *not to contend with others on account of their faith,* or systems of religion, but pursue a steady course. This I deliver by way of commandment, and all who observe it not will pull down persecution upon their heads, while those who do shall always be filled with the Holy Ghost; this I pronounce as a prophecy.

Joseph Smith, Jr.; italics added

Home teaching is missionary work to the member. Missionary work is home teaching to the nonmember.

Harold B. Lee

Our missionaries are going forth in different nations, . . . the Standard of Truth has been erected; no unhallowed hand can stop the work from progressing; persecutions may rage, mobs may combine, armies may assemble, calumny may defame, but the truth of God will go forth boldly, nobly, and independent, till it has penetrated every continent, visited every clime, swept every country, and sounded in every ear, till the purposes of God shall be accomplished, and the Great Jehovah shall say the work is done.

Joseph Smith, Jr.
from the Wentworth Letter

Our missionaries are not salesmen, with wares to peddle; rather, they are servants of the Most High God, with a testimony to bear, truth to teach, and souls to save.

Thomas S. Monson

And ye shall go forth in the power of my Spirit, preaching my gospel, two by two, in my name, lifting up your voices as with the sound of a trump, declaring my word like unto angels of God.

Doctrine & Covenants 42:6

As certainly as there is a God in heaven, this gospel will go forth unto the ends of the earth.

Gordon B. Hinckley

Go ye therefore, and teach all nations, baptizing them in the name of the Father, and of the Son, and of the Holy Ghost.

Matthew 28:19

Go forth among the Lamanites, thy brethren, and establish my word; . . . and I will make an instrument of thee in my hands unto the salvation of many souls.

Alma 17:11

Therefore, strengthen your brethren in all your conversation, in all your prayers, in all your exhortations, and in all your doings.

Doctrine & Covenants 108:7

The true way to serve the Lord is through service to man. We should be extremely happy when serving in His church.

David O. McKay

In the mouth of two or three witnesses every word may be established.

Matthew 18:16

I know that which the Lord hath commanded me, and I glory in it. I do not glory of myself, but I glory in that which the Lord hath commanded me; yea, and this is my glory, that perhaps I may be an instrument in the hands of God to bring some soul to repentance; and this is my joy.

Alma 29:9

In the service of the Lord, it is not *where*, but *how* you serve.

J. Reuben Clark, Jr.

Go forth and preach the Gospel, gain an experience, learn wisdom and walk humbly before your God, that you may receive the Holy Ghost to guide you and direct you and teach you all things past, present and to come. Go trusting in God, and continue to trust in Him and He will open your way and multiply [his blessings] upon you.

Brigham Young

Go ye therefore, and teach all nations, baptizing them in the name of the Father, and of the Son, and of the Holy Ghost:
Teaching them to observe all things whatsoever I have commanded you: and lo, I am with you alway, even unto the end of the world. Amen.

Matthew 28:19-20

Let him know, that he which converteth the sinner from the error of his way shall save a soul from death, and shall hide a multitude of sins.

James 5:20

The time now is close at hand, and we are under condemnation by the Lord. . . . We need to FLOOD THE EARTH with the Book of Mormon.

Ezra Taft Benson

After these things the Lord appointed other seventy also, and sent them two and two before his face into every city and place, whither he himself would come.
Therefore said he unto them, The harvest truly is great, but the labourers are few: pray ye therefore the Lord of the harvest, that he would send forth labourers into his harvest.

Luke 10: 1-2

WHERE SHALL I WORK TODAY?

Master, where shall I work today?
My love flowed warm and free.
He pointed out a tiny spot
And said, tend that for me.

I answered quickly, oh no, not there,
Not any one could see
No matter how well my work was done;
Not that little spot for me.

When He spoke He was not stern,
But He answered me tenderly,
Little one, search that heart of thine;
Are you working for them or for me?
Nazareth was just a little place.
And so was Galilee.

Anonymous

The more people you see, and see well,
   the more you'll teach.
The more people you teach, and teach well,
   the more you'll baptize.
The more people you baptize well, the more
   you'll see turning up in the mission field, at
   church, in the temple, and in the celestial
   kingdom.

Ricardo Diaz

But sanctify the Lord God in your hearts: and be
ready always to give an answer to every man that
asketh you a reason of the hope that is in you.

1 Peter 3:15

Make your life a mission, not an intermission.

Arnold H. Glasgow

OBEDIENCE

You cannot do wrong and feel right.

Ezra Taft Benson

If you will that I give unto you a place in the celestial world, you must prepare yourselves by doing the things which I have commanded you and required of you.

Doctrine & Covenants 78:7

Inasmuch as ye will keep my commandments ye shall prosper in the land.

Jarom 1:9 (repeated 22 times in the Book of Mormon)

I will go and do the things which the Lord hath commanded, for I know that the Lord giveth no commandments unto the children of men, save he shall prepare a way for them that they may accomplish the thing which he commandeth them.

1 Nephi 3:7

Be faithful and diligent in keeping the commandments of God, and I will encircle thee in the arms of my love.

Doctrine & Covenants 6:20

And thou shalt love the Lord thy God with all thine heart, and with all thy soul, and with all thy might.

Deuteronomy 6:5

I have no greater joy than to hear that my children walk in truth.

3 John 1:4

If ye love me, keep my commandments.

John 14:15

For verily I say unto you, blessed is he that keepeth my commandments, whether in life or in death; and he that is faithful in tribulation, the reward of the same is greater in the kingdom of heaven.

Doctrine & Covenants 58:2

I, the Lord, am bound when ye do what I say; but when ye do not what I say, ye have no promise.

Doctrine & Covenants 82:10

Let no man break the laws of the land, for he that keepeth the laws of God hath no need to break the laws of the land.

Doctrine & Covenants 58:21

O, remember, my son, and learn wisdom in thy youth; yea, learn in thy youth to keep the commandments of God.

Alma 37:35

If you keep my commandments and endure to the end you shall have eternal life, which gift is the greatest of all the gifts of God.

Doctrine & Covenants 14:7

And this is love, that we walk after his commandments.

2 John 1:6

OUR RELATIONSHIP WITH HEAVENLY FATHER / OUR HEAVENLY FATHER'S PLAN

For behold, this is my work and my glory—to bring to pass the immortality and eternal life of man.

Moses 1:39

Know ye that the Lord he is God: it is he that hath made us, and not we ourselves; we are his people, and the sheep of his pasture.

Psalms 100:3

If you would bless your fellow man the most, then you must put the First Commandment first.

Ezra Taft Benson

Though the heavens and the earth pass away, my word shall not pass away, but shall all be fulfilled.

Doctrine & Covenants 1:38

Eye hath not seen, nor ear heard, neither have entered into the heart of man, the things which God hath prepared for them that love him.

1 Corinthians 2:9

For the eternal purposes of the Lord shall roll on, until all his promises shall be fulfilled.

Mormon 8:22

Blessed are all they that put their trust in him.

Psalms 2:12

But God is faithful, who will not suffer you to be tempted above that ye are able; but will with the temptation also make a way to escape, that ye may be able to bear it.

1 Corinthians 10:13

Even if the Church weren't true, it would still be the best way to raise a righteous family unto our Heavenly Father. This is the "common sense" approach to understanding the gospel.

Gifford Nielson

The highest ideal of man is the will of God.

Anonymous

OUR RELATIONSHIP WITH COMPANIONS / OTHERS

That two men may be real friends, they must have opposite opinions, similar principles, and different loves and hatreds.

François Rene de Chateaubriand

Seek no friend to make him useful, for that is the negation of friendship; but seek him that you may be useful, for this is of friendship's essence.

Henry Wallace

You can make more friends in two months by becoming interested in other people than you can in two years by trying to get other people interested in you.

Dale Carnegie

Make friendship a habit and you will always have friends.

Jacob M. Braude

When you judge others you do not define them. You define yourself.

Anonymous

We must not lose faith in humanity. Humanity is an ocean; if a few drops of the ocean are dirty, the ocean does not become dirty.

Mohandas K. Gandhi

For the Lord seeth not as man seeth; for man looketh on the outward appearance, but the Lord looketh on the heart.

1 Samuel 16:7

If we are not rejoicing and edifying one another in all our conversations, then we are doing something wrong.

Eric Huntsman

Telling your troubles always helps. The world's indifference makes you mad enough to keep on fighting. After all, 80% of the people don't care about the fix you've gotten yourself into, and the other 20% are glad you got what's coming!

Allan Clements

Half the secret of getting along with people is consideration of their views; the other half is tolerance in one's own views.

Daniel Frohman

Deal with the faults of others as gently as with your own.

Chinese proverb

The responsibility of tolerance lies with those tho have the wider vision.

George Eliot

Judge not, that ye be not judged.
For with that judgment ye judge, ye shall be judged.

Matthew 7:1-2

Judge not, and ye shall not be judged: condemn not, and ye shall not be condemned: forgive, and ye shall be forgiven.

Luke 6:37

Prejudices . . . are most difficult to eradicate from the heart whose soil has never been loosened or fertilized by education; they grow there, firm as weeds among stones.

Charlotte Brontë

If you treat a man as he is, he will remain as he is, but if you treat him as if he were what he ought to be, and could be, he will become what he ought to be, and should be.

Goethe

Rebuke not an elder, but intreat him as a father; and the younger men as brethren.

1 Timothy 5:1

Cultivate the mutual understanding of anyone
you have to get along with.

Dwight D. Eisenhower

OUR PATH IN LIFE

You cannot control the length of your life, but you can control its breadth, depth and height.

Anonymous

Life is the acceptance of responsibilities, or their evasion. It is the business of meeting obligations or avoiding them. To every man the choice is continually being offered, and by the manner of his choosing you may fairly measure him.

Ben Ames Williams

The secret of life is not to do what one likes, but to try to like what one has to do.

Dinah Muloch Craik

Life is not a rigid business of being, but a lively process of becoming.

Ford Lewis

The life of every man is a diary in which he means to write one story and writes another; and his humblest hour is when he compares the volume as it is with what he had hoped to make it.

James M. Barrie

Life is what happens to you while you're busy doing something else.

Anonymous

One of the most tragic things I know about human nature is that all of us tend to put off living. We are all dreaming of some magical rose garden over the horizon—instead of enjoying the roses that are blooming outside our windows today.

Dale Carnegie

Life is a quarry, out of which we have to mold and chisel and complete a character.

Goethe

Be not deceived; God is not mocked: for whatsoever a man soweth, that shall he also reap.

Galatians 6:7

Wherefore, be of good cheer, and do not fear, for I the Lord am with you, and will stand by you.

Doctrine & Covenants 68:6

PATIENCE / LONG-SUFFERING

Be faithful unto the end, and lo, I am with you.

Doctrine & Covenants 31:13

My people must be tried in all things, . . . he that will not bear chastisement is not worthy of my kingdom.

Doctrine & Covenants 136:31

Be patient in afflictions, for thou shalt have many.

Doctrine & Covenants 24:8

No ray of sunshine is ever lost,
But the green which it awakes into existence
Needs time to sprout,
And it is not always granted to the sower
To see the harvest.
All work that is worth anything
Is done in faith.

Albert Schweitzer

In the world ye shall have tribulation: but be of good cheer; I have overcome the world.

John 16:33

No man knows how much he can endure until he must. Strength, patience and ability increase with necessity.

Richard L. Evans

Sometimes we take credit for being patient when we are only putting off doing something unpleasant.

Anonymous

Blessed are all they who are persecuted for my name's sake, for theirs is the kingdom of heaven.

3 Nephi 12:10

He is a fool who cannot be angry; but he is a wise man who *will* not.

Anonymous

Patience is a necessary ingredient of genius.

Benjamin Disraeli

When you are an anvil, be patient. When a hammer, strike.

Arabian proverb

Night never had the last word. The dawn is always invincible.

Hugh B. Brown

My son, peace be unto thy soul; thine adversity and thine afflictions shall be but a small moment; And then, if thou endure it well, God shall exalt thee on high.

Doctrine & Covenants 121:7-8

PERSISTENCE / OVERCOMING OBSTACLES

That which we persist in doing becomes easier—not that the nature of the thing has changed, but that our ability to do it has increased.

Heber J. Grant

Second wind is only to a very small degree a question of breathing power. It is, rather, the response of the vital forces to a will that refuses to heed their first grumbling protests.

Stewart Edward White

With ordinary talent and extraordinary perseverance, all things are attainable.

Thomas Fowell Buxton

He that wrestles with us strengthens our nerves
and sharpens our skill; our opponent is our
helper, because it is only through resistance that
we gain strength.

Edmund Burke

Some men can get results if kindly encouraged,
but give me the kind that do things in spite of hell.

Elbert Hubbard

Emotional maturity is the ability to stick to a job and to struggle through until it is finished; to endure unpleasantness, discomfort and frustration; to give more than is asked for or required; to size up and make independent decisions; to work under authority and to cooperate with others; to defer to time, other persons, and to circumstances.

Edwin A. Strecker

Some men succeed because they are destined to, but most because they are determined to.

Anonymous

People do not lack strength. They lack will.

Anonymous

A journey of a thousand miles begins with a single step. But it takes *courage* and *persistence* to make all the rest.

Chip Cooper

It isn't enough to put your best foot forward; you have to follow through with your other foot, too.

Jacob M. Braude

Hard things are put in our way—not to stop us, but to call out our courage and strength.

Anonymous

Many men owe the grandeur of their lives to their tremendous difficulties.

Walter Spurgeon

For our light affliction, which is but for a moment, worketh for us a far more exceeding and eternal weight of glory.

2 Corinthians 4:17

Diligence is the mother of good fortune, and God gives abundantly to industry. So plow deep while the sluggards sleep, and you shall have corn to sell and to keep.

Benjamin Franklin

I can do all things through Christ which strengtheneth me.

Philippians 4:13

Let us not be weary in well doing: for in due season we shall reap, if we faint not.

Galatians 6:9

Wherefore, be not weary in well-doing, for ye are laying the foundation of a great work. And out of small things proceedeth that which is great.

Doctrine & Covenants 64:33

Quitters never win. Winners never quit.

Virginia Hutchinson

The harder the conflict, the more glorious the triumph. What we obtain too cheaply we esteem too lightly.

Thomas Paine

It is for us to make the effort. The result is always in God's hands.

Mohandas K. Gandhi

Adversity is the midwife of genius.

Napoleon Bonaparte

Progress in any age results only from the fact that there are some men and women who refuse to believe that what they know to be right cannot be accomplished.

Russell W. Davenport

These are the times that try men's souls. Tyranny, like hell, is not easily conquered: our consolation is that the harder the conflict, the more glorious the triumph.

Thomas Paine, 1775

The nearer a person approaches the Lord, the greater power will be manifest by the Adversary to prevent the accomplishment of his purpose.

Heber C. Kimball

You must have long-range goals to keep you from being frustrated by short-range failures.

Charles C. Noble

An obstacle is often an unrecognized opportunity. When a man wages war against his weakness, this is the most holy war he can ever enter . . . and the joy of accomplishment is the most exquisite.

Marion G. Romney

The honor of the conquest is rated by the difficulty.

Michel de Montaign

Follow through: stopping at third base adds no more to the score than striking out.

Alexander Animator

Diligence is the mother of good fortune.

Miguel de Cervantes

As a gem cannot be polished without friction, neither can a man be perfected without trials.

Confucius

Skill and confidence are an unconquered army.

George Herbert

From the eternal perspective, it's not whether I win the battle or not that counts—it's the way I kept on fighting.

Spencer W. Kimball

The most important thing in your calling isn't the numbers or the positions, it's the *doing your best*.

Jacob de Jager

You can't be brave if you've only had wonderful things happen to you.

Mary Tyler Moore

Great works are performed not by strength, but by perseverance.

Samuel Johnson

TRIUMPH usually comes from putting a little more "umph" into your "try."

Quoted by Thomas S. Monson

We are not measured by the trials we meet—only by those we overcome.

Spencer W. Kimball

There is no education like adversity.

Benjamin Disraeli

Tough times don't last—tough people do.

Anonymous

PRAYER

When we pray unto the Father in the name of Jesus for specific personal things, we should feel in the very depths of our souls that we are willing to subject our petitions to the will of our Father in Heaven.

Marion G. Romney

Let the words of my mouth, and the meditation of my heart, be acceptable in thy sight, O Lord, my strength, and my redeemer.

Psalms 19:14

Who rises from prayer a better man, his prayer is answered.

George Meredith

It is better in prayer to have a heart without words, than words without heart.

Mahatma Gandhi

Create in me a clean heart, O God; and renew a right spirit within me.
Cast me not away from thy presence; and take not thy holy spirit from me.
Restore unto me the joy of thy salvation; and uphold me with thy free spirit.

Psalms 51:10-12

Do not pray for tasks equal to your powers. Pray for powers equal to your tasks.

Thomas S. Monson

When a need is highest, God is nighest.

Hebrew proverb

Pray as if everything depended on God, and then work as if everything depended on you.

Francis Cardinal Spellman

Prayer is the key that unlocks every door of difficulty. But a key is not to be used only once a day; it is to be used every time you come to a locked door.

George B. Tullidge

Prayer is not a substitute for work; it is a some-times desperate effort to work further and to be efficient beyond the range of one's powers. It is not the lazy who are most inclined to prayer; those pray most who care most, and who, having worked hard, find it intolerable to be defeated.

George Santayana

Prayer isn't something that we do, and then stop doing. If we are really praying, we carry our prayers with us wherever we go; it is a discipline. It is an art that can be learned. Whenever a thought comes to you, that thought can immedi-ately be translated into prayer.

William Fitch

If any of you lack wisdom, let him ask of God, that giveth to all men liberally, and upbraideth not; and it shall be given him.

James 1:5

God is greater than your greatest need.

C. Mervyn Maxwell

Prayer keeps a man from sin, and sin keeps a man from prayer.

Brigham Young

Prayer is a conversation with God, but prayer is no substitute for work.

Henry D. Moyle

Rejoice evermore. Pray without ceasing.

1 Thessalonians 5:16-17

Every night I turn all my troubles over to God . . .
He'll be up all night anyway.

Jim Humphrey

But behold, I say unto you that ye must pray
always, and not faint; that ye must not perform
any thing unto the Lord save in the first place ye
shall pray unto the Father in the name of Christ,
that he will consecrate thy performance unto
thee, that thy performance may be for the welfare
of thy soul.

2 Nephi 32:9

Do not shout in your prayer, nor say it under your breath; set a course in between.

The Koran

Is any sick among you? let him call for the elders of the church; and let them pray over him, anointing him with oil in the name of the Lord: And the prayer of faith shall save the sick, and the Lord shall raise him up; and if he have committed sins, they shall be forgiven him. Confess your faults one to another, and pray one for another, that ye may be healed. The effectual fervent prayer of a righteous man availeth much.

James 5:14-16

All victory and glory is brought to pass unto you through your diligence, faithfulness, and prayers of faith.

Doctrine & Covenants 103:36

A man of faith does not bargain or stipulate with God.

Mahatma Gandhi

On those occasions when you *don't* feel like praying, you should get on your knees and pray until you *do* feel like praying.

Brigham Young

PREPAREDNESS

If ye are prepared ye shall not fear.

Doctrine & Covenants 38:30

If we exercise now, how much stronger we will be when the test comes!

William James

Organize yourselves; prepare every needful thing; and establish a house, even a house of prayer, a house of fasting, a house of faith, a house of learning, a house of glory, a house of order, a house of God.

Doctrine & Covenants 88:119

Forewarned is forearmed. To be prepared is half the victory.

Miguel de Cervantes

No man not inspired can make a good speech without preparation.

Daniel Webster

There is no security on this earth. There is only opportunity.

Douglas MacArthur

The trouble with an opportunity is that it always comes disguised as hard work.

Will Rogers

It is not given to us to see the end from the beginning. But the *habits* we develop will eventually determine what that end will be.

R. Dale Jeffery

Luck comes to those who are first prepared. For how shall one catch the fish without first a hook or a net? So gather bait, and let your hook always be cast: for in the stream when you shall least expect it, there will be fish!

Anonymous

Opportunity knocks as often as a man has an ear trained to hear it, an eye trained to see it, a hand trained to grasp it, and a head trained to utilize it.

Andrew Carnegie

When one door closes another opens, but we often look so long and so regretfully upon the closed door that we do not see the one which has opened for us.

Alexander Graham Bell

Get your tools ready: God will find the work.

Anonymous

When schemes are laid in advance, it is surprising how often the circumstances fit in with them.

Sir William Osler

A man who is young in age may still be old and experienced, if he has lost no time.

Sir Francis Bacon

The essential thing is not to find, but to absorb what we find.

Paul Valers

Desire can be measured through preparation.

Barton Thacker

You seldom get what you go after unless you know in advance what you want. Indecision has often given an advantage to the other fellow because he did his thinking beforehand.

Maurice Switzer

Live neither in the past nor in the future, but let each day's work absorb all your interest, energy and enthusiasm. The best preparation for tomorrow is to do today's work superbly well.

Sir William Osler

A wise man will make more opportunities than he finds.

Sir Francis Bacon

Wishing consumes just as much time and energy as planning does. Worrying consumes more.

Anonymous

Most people don't plan to fail—they just fail to plan.

Anonymous

Any dog inside a fence will bark and clamor to get out. But once they are out, most dogs run around for a while, sniff out the territory, then sit down by the fence. This is because they *focused only on getting out* and never thought of what to do *after* they got out.

Many humans are the same way. We say, "I can't wait to get out of high school," or "I just want out of this relationship," or "I'm just going to get through college as fast as I can." In a missionary sense, we might say, "I can't wait to get home/ out of this area," or "Just wait until I get my new companion."

But what are we doing now? Are we planning what to do and preparing our souls for the trials we'll encounter on the other side? If not, then are we any different from the dog?

R. Dale Jeffery (Journal entry, Korea, 1995)

I respect the man who knows distinctly what he wishes. The greater part of all mischief in the world arises from the fact that men do not sufficiently understand their own aims. They have undertaken to build a tower and spend no more labor on the foundation than would be necessary to erect a hut.

Goethe

Act before there is a problem. Bring order before there is disorder.

The Tao Te Ching

A danger foreseen is half avoided.

Thomas Fuller

PRIESTHOOD / PRIESTHOOD RESPONSIBILITIES

For whoso is faithful unto the obtaining these two priesthoods of which I have spoken, and the magnifying their calling, are sanctified by the Spirit unto the renewing of their bodies.

They become the sons of Moses and of Aaron and the seed of Abraham, and the church and kingdom, and the elect of God.

And this is according to the oath and covenant which belongeth to the priesthood.

Doctrine & Covenants 84:33-34, 39

No power or influence can or ought to be maintained by virtue of the priesthood, only by persuasion, by long-suffering, by gentleness and meekness, and by love unfeigned.

Doctrine & Covenants 121:41

He commandeth that there shall be no priestcrafts; for, behold, priestcrafts are that men preach and set themselves up for a light unto the world, that they may get gain and praise of the world; but they seek not the welfare of Zion.

2 Nephi 26:29

The rights of the priesthood are inseparably connected with the powers of heaven, and . . . the powers of heaven cannot be controlled nor handled only upon the principles of righteousness. That they may be conferred upon us, it is true; but when we undertake to cover our sins, or to gratify our pride, our vain ambition, or to exercise control or dominion or compulsion upon the souls of the children of men, in any degree of unrighteousness, behold, the heavens withdraw themselves; the Spirit of the Lord is grieved; and when it is withdrawn, Amen to the priesthood or the authority of that man.

Doctrine & Covenants
121:36-37

And whatsoever thou shalt bind on earth shall be bound in heaven: and whatsoever thou shalt loose on earth shall be loosed in heaven.

Matthew 16:19

And no man taketh this honour unto himself, but he that is called of God, as was Aaron.

Hebrews 5:4

As a priesthood holder, are you ready in your heart to exercise those rights and responsibilities and to provide priesthood service, at any time? Are you prepared both physically and spiritually to give a blessing or lead a meeting or give a talk or testimony whenever you're called upon? Are you doing the right things in your personal life so you're ready to stand as a witness of Christ at all times, at all places, and in all things?

If you're not, then you should be. You're the one with the stewardship, after all, and this is no small job.

Barton Thacker

The duty of the elders, priests, teachers, deacons, and members of the church of Christ—An apostle is an elder, and it is his calling to baptize; And to ordain other elders, priests, teachers, and deacons;

And to administer bread and wine—the emblems of the flesh and blood of Christ—

And to confirm those who are baptized into the church, by the laying on of hands for the baptism of fire and the Holy Ghost, according to the scriptures;

And to teach, expound, exhort, baptize, and watch over the church;

And to confirm the church by the laying on of the hands, and the giving of the Holy Ghost;

And to take the lead of all meetings.

The elders are to conduct the meetings as they are led by the Holy Ghost, according to the commandments and revelations of God.

Doctrine & Covenants
20: 38-45

PROGRESS AND PROGRESSION

I will go anywhere—provided it is forward.

Dr. David Livingstone

Our only concern should be to do better than we did yesterday. Step by step is the law of growth. God does not expect the acorn to be a mighty oak before it has been a sapling.

George E. Carpenter

Progress depends upon what we are, rather than upon what we may encounter. One man is stopped by a sapling lying across the road which he carefully avoids or steps over. A second will push it out of the way for the benefit of others that follow. A third man, passing the same way, picks up the hindrance and converts it into a help in crossing the brook just ahead.

Jonathan Trumbull

I don't think much of a man who is not wiser today than he was yesterday.

Abraham Lincoln

When we're through changing, we're through.

Bruce Barton

Progress, or perish.

B. H. Roberts

I find the great thing in this world is not so much where we stand as in what direction we are moving: To reach the port of Heaven, we must sail sometimes with the wind and sometimes against it—but we must sail, and not drift, nor lie at anchor.

Oliver Wendell Holmes

Improvement always comes with a price.

Anonymous

Most people are in favor of progress; it's the *change* they don't like.

Anonymous

Never discourage anyone . . . who continually makes progress, no matter how slow.

Plato

The Kingdom of God, or nothing.

John Taylor

Have confidence that if you have done a little thing well, you can do a bigger thing well, too.

Moorfield Storey

If we are to be stretching and growing throughout eternity, why should we think God would ever give us talents and allotments to be content with here on earth?

Neal A. Maxwell

To be forever reaching out, to remain unsatisfied, is the key to spiritual progress.

Arden Engebretsen

Satan also works line upon line.

Anonymous

Progress consists largely of learning to apply laws and principles which have already existed.

John Allan May

PURITY / INTEGRITY

Who shall ascend into the hill of the Lord? or who shall stand in his holy place?
He that hath clean hands, and a pure heart; who hath not lifted up his soul unto vanity, nor sworn deceitfully.

Psalms 24:3-4

We are tools in the hands of God. We must be properly crafted, properly aligned and well-maintained so that we can be of full use to our Heavenly Father.

John Holman

For I will raise up unto myself a pure people, that will serve me in righteousness.

Doctrine & Covenants 100:16

And the Lord called his people Zion, because they were of one heart and one mind, and dwelt in righteousness; and there was no poor among them.

Moses 7:18

Be what you are. This is the first step toward becoming better than you are.

Julius Hare

True bravery is shown by performing with no witness what one might be capable of doing before all the world.

Françios de la Rouchefoucald

Turn away if you must, but don't back down or acquiesce in silence if your integrity is at stake. Loss of integrity diminishes everybody's opinion of you, including your own.

Hyrum Plaas

Truth is violated by falsehood, and it may be equally outraged by silence.

Ammian

Some people throw away a bushel of truth because it contains a grain of error, while others swallow a bushel of error because it contains a grain of truth.

Anonymous

There is a difference between innocence and virtue. To be innocent is to be not guilty; but to be virtuous is to overcome our evil feelings and intentions.

William Penn

The way to gain a good reputation is to endeavor to be what you desire to appear.

Socrates

The chief vice of many people consists not in doing evil, but in permitting it.

Anonymous

When in doubt, speak the truth.

Mark Twain

I do the very best I know how; the very best I can; and I mean to keep doing so until the end. If the end brings me out all right, what is said against me won't amount to anything.

Abraham Lincoln

Yea, come unto Christ, and be perfected in him, and deny yourselves of all ungodliness; . . . and love God with all your might, mind and strength.

Moroni 10:32

Blessed are all the pure in heart, for they shall see God.

3 Nephi 12:8

Character is the ability to follow through with the objective or commitment long after the original motivation has passed.

Larry Beckham

Do not wish to be anything but what you are—
and try to be that perfectly.

St. Francis de Sales

A man's own character is the arbiter of his
fortune.

Plubius

Rumor travels faster, but it doesn't stay put as
long as truth.

Will Rogers

Let virtue garnish thy thoughts unceasingly; then
shall thy confidence wax strong in the presence of
God; and the doctrine of the priesthood shall
distil upon thy soul as the dews from heaven.

Doctrine & Covenants 121:45

Sanctify yourselves therefore, and be ye holy: for I am the Lord your God.

Leviticus 20:7

REVELATION

Yea, he that repenteth and exerciseth faith, and bringeth forth good works, and prayeth continually without ceasing—unto such it is given to know the mysteries of God; yea, unto such it shall be given to reveal things which never have been revealed.

Alma 26:22

Yea, behold, I will tell you in your mind and in your heart, by the Holy Ghost, which shall come upon you and which shall dwell in your heart.
Now, behold, this is the spirit of revelation; behold, this is the spirit by which Moses brought the children of Israel through the Red Sea on dry ground.

Doctrine & Covenants 8:2-3

Those days were never to be forgotten—to sit under the sound of a voice dictated by the inspiration of heaven, awakened the utmost gratitude of this bosom! Day after day I continued, uninterrupted, to write from his mouth as he translated . . . the history or record called "the Book of Mormon."

Oliver Cowdery

The Lord will never permit me or any other man who stands as president of this church to lead you astray.

Wilford Woodruff

Eye hath not seen, nor ear heard, neither have entered into the heart of man, the things which God hath prepared for them that love him.
But God hath revealed them unto us by his Spirit; for the Spirit searcheth all things, yea, the deep things of God.

1 Corinthians 2:9-10

Surely the Lord God will do nothing, but he revealeth his secret unto his servants the prophets.

Amos 3:7

I will fulfill all that which I have caused to be spoken by the mouth of my holy prophets.

3 Nephi 1:13

Search these commandments, for they are true and faithful, and the prophecies and promises which are in them shall all be fulfilled.

What I the Lord have spoken, I have spoken, and I excuse not myself; and though the heavens and the earth pass away, my word shall not pass away, but shall all be fulfilled, whether by mine own voice or by the voice of my servants, it is the same.

Doctrine & Covenants 1:37-38

For thou shalt go to all that I shall send thee, and whatsoever I command thee thou shalt speak.

Jeremiah 1:7

Seek not to declare my word, but seek first to obtain my word, and then shall your tongue be loosed; then, if you desire, you shall have my Spirit and my word, yea, the power of God unto the convincing of men.

Doctrine & Covenants 11:21

And thou shalt continue in calling upon God in my name, and writing the things which shall be given thee by the Comforter, and expounding all scriptures unto the church.
And it shall be given thee in the very moment what thou shalt speak and write.

Doctrine & Covenants 24:5-6

Open thy mouth, and it shall be filled, and I will give thee utterance.

Moses 6:32

He that receiveth the word by the Spirit of truth receiveth it as it is preached by the Spirit of truth. Wherefore, he that preacheth and he that receiveth, understand one another, and both are edified and rejoice together.

Doctrine & Covenants
50:21-22

REPENTANCE, FORGIVENESS, FAILURE, EXPERIENCE

The only way to cure a bad conscience is to stop doing what we shouldn't do, and start doing what we should do.

Richard L. Evans

When I do good, I feel good. When I don't do good, I don't feel good.

Abraham Lincoln

Create in me a clean heart, O God; and renew a right spirit within me.
Cast me not away from thy presence; and take not thy holy spirit from me.
Restore unto me the joy of thy salvation; and uphold me with thy free spirit.

Psalms 51:10-12

You can't be right by doing wrong, and you can't go wrong by doing right.

Thomas S. Monson

A fault confessed is a fault redressed; a fault once denied is twice committed.

Ancient proverb

In pardoning, we rise above those who insult us.

Napoleon Bonaparte

Rationalizing is
    the bringing of one's ideals down
                    to the level of one's conduct.

Repentance is
    the bringing of one's conduct up
                    to the level of one's ideals.

Unknown

To err is human; to forgive, divine.

Alexander Pope

I, the Lord, will forgive whom I will forgive, but of you it is required to forgive all men.

Doctrine & Covenants 64:10

"I can forgive, but I cannot forget," is only another way of saying, "I cannot forgive."

Henry Ward Beecher

To err is human,
To forgive takes restraint;
To forget you forgave
Is the mark of a Saint.

Suzanne Douglas

For, if ye forgive men their trespasses your heavenly Father will also forgive you.

3 Nephi 13:14

It is better to go out and make new mistakes than to repeat the old ones over and over again. When you feel uneasiness, and bewail misfortunes, you should examine the roots from which they spring—even down to your own folly, your own pride, or your own mistempered fancy. Do not murmur, therefore, but correct yourself.

Dandemis

You cannot do wrong and feel right.

Ezra Taft Benson

The man who never makes mistakes loses a great many chances to learn something.

Anonymous

Regret for the things we did can be tempered by time; it is regret for the things we did not do that is inconsolable.

Sydney J. Harris

Defeat may serve as well as victory to shake the soul and let the glory out.

Edwin Markham

To receive a stab is to be wounded; but to forgive and forget it, is the cure.

Rev. William Scott Downey

Adam fell, but he got right back up.

Anonymous

It is all right to forget your mistakes, as long as you remember their lessons.

Anonymous

Don't blame the typewriter when you misspell the word.

Anonymous

Show me a man who doesn't know the meaning of the word "fail," and I'll show you a man who ought to buy a dictionary.

Albert Einstein

Behold, I say unto you, wickedness never was happiness.

Alma 41:10

It is never too late to be what you might have been.

George Eliot

You become strong by defying defeat, and by turning loss to gain and failure to success.

Napoleon Bonaparte

There are two kinds of failures: The man who will do nothing he is told, and the man who will do nothing else.

Perle Thompson

Reading is not a substitute for experience; neither is experience a substitute for reading.

Aldous Huxley

Just because we have taken one step down a wrong road is no reason why we have to take two.

Richard L. Evans

Bad men excuse their faults. Good men abandon them.

Anonymous

When you pay for experience, make sure you keep the receipt!

Tyler Brinkman

Self-Discipline /
Self-Control, Habits,
Time Management

No one is free who is not a master of himself.

William Shakespeare

The first and best victory is to conquer self.

Plato

It is often said that a man's personal religion grows out of the uses to which he puts his moments of solitude. A sure mark of an irreligious person is one who hates to ever be alone, who must be constantly amused by radio, television, canasta or idle companionship. Such shows the lack of self-discipline and self-determination.

Gilbert M. Holloway

Our lives are what our thoughts create.

James Allen

For as he thinketh in his heart, so is he.

Proverbs 23:7

No man is free who is not master of his soul and controller of his spirit.

Thomas Crombie

The way we are going to think tomorrow depends largely on what we are thinking today.

David Leslie Brown

Worry a little bit every day and in a lifetime you will lose a couple of years. If something is wrong, fix it if you can. But train yourself not to worry. Worry never fixes anything.

Ole Helgerson

There is no use worrying about things over which you have no control, and if you have control, you can do something about them instead of worrying.

Stanley C. Allyn

In the beginning, habits are like cobwebs. In the end they are cables.

Chinese proverb

You can often gauge a man's ambition by whether he hates his alarm clock or considers it his best friend.

Thomas Edison

The great end of education is to discipline rather than to furnish the mind; to train it to the use of its own powers, rather than fill it with the accumulation of others.

Tryon Edwards

'Tis easier to suppress the first desire, than to satisfy all that follow it.

Benjamin Franklin

Self-control may be developed in precisely the same manner as we tone up a weak muscle—by little exercises day by day.

W. G. Jordan

Silence is not always tact, and it is tact that is golden, not silence.

Samuel Butler

It often shows a fine command of language to say nothing.

Anonymous

The best answer to anger is silence.

German proverb

One minute of keeping your mouth shut is worth an hour of explanation.

Anonymous

Use boldness, but not overbearance; and also see that ye bridle all your passions, that ye may be filled with love; see that ye refrain from idleness.

Alma 38:12

If you wish to succeed in managing and controlling others—learn to manage and control yourself.

William Boetcker

None is deemed to be free who has not perfect self-command.

Pythagoras

What we do upon some great occasion will probably depend on what we already are; and what we are will be the result of previous years of self-discipline.

Henry Louis Liddon

SERVICE

When ye are in the service of your fellow beings ye are only in the service of your God.

Mosiah 2:17

It is high time the ideal of success should be replaced with the ideal of service.

Albert Einstein

Do all the good you can,
By all the means you can,
In all the ways you can,
In all the places you can,
To all the people you can,
As long as ever you can.

John Wesley

And whosoever shall compel thee to go a mile, go with him twain.

Matthew 5:41

Verily I say unto you, Inasmuch as ye have done it unto one of the least of these my brethren, ye have done it unto me.

Matthew 25:40

For inasmuch as ye do it unto the least of these, ye do it unto me.

Doctrine & Covenants 42:38

Service makes men competent.

Lyman Abbott

Bear ye one another's burdens, and so fulfil the law of Christ.

Galatians 6:2

Therefore, O ye that embark in the service of God, see that ye serve him with all your heart, might, mind and strength, that ye may stand blameless before God at the last day.

Doctrine & Covenants 4:2

What we have done for ourselves alone dies with us. What we have done for others and the world remains and is immortal.

Alexander Pope

The noblest service comes from nameless hands, and the best servant does his work unseen.

Anonymous

But ye will teach them to walk in the ways of truth and soberness; ye will teach them to love one another, and to serve one another.

Mosiah 4:15

Pure religion and undefiled before God and the Father is this, To visit the fatherless and widows in their affliction, and to keep [thyself] unspotted from the world.

James 1:27

Let us not be weary in well doing; for in due season we shall reap, if we faint not.

Galatians 6:9

A man has no more religion than he acts out in his life.

Henry Ward Beecher

What a great difference there is between giving advice and lending a hand!

Anonymous

You have not lived today until you have done something for someone who can never repay you.

James M. Braude

When sowing seeds
Of friendly deeds,
The less you keep
The more you reap.

Christopher Bannister

Life is like a game of tennis; the player who serves
well seldom loses.

Anonymous

There's a destiny that makes us brothers,
None goes his way alone.
All that we send into the lives of others
Will come back into our own.

Edwin Markham

Service is the price we pay for living on this earth.

N. Eldon Tanner

Doing good to others is not a duty. It is a joy, for
it increases your own health and happiness.

Zoroaster

It is one of the most beautiful compensations of this life that no man can sincerely try to help another without helping himself.

Emerson

TALENTS / CREATIVITY

Use what talents you possess. The woods would be very silent if no birds sang there except those that sang best.

Henry Van Dyke

When we can learn to use the talents God has given us to their fullest extent, then what we can accomplish is only limited by what God will allow.

Larry Beckham

What makes men of genius, or rather what inspires their work, is not new ideas but the obsession that what has already been done is not enough.

Eugene Delacroix

Genius is initiative on fire.

Holbrook Jackson

The Lord doesn't ask about our *inabilities* or *abilities*. He only asks about our *availabilities*. If we show our *dependability*, He will help us in our *capability*.

Neal A. Maxwell

No lions are ever caught in mousetraps. To catch lions you must think in terms of lions, not in terms of mice. Your mind is always creating traps of one kind or another, and what you catch depends on the thinking you do. It is your thinking that attracts you to what you receive.

Thomas Dreier

Knowledge comes by taking things apart: *analysis*. But wisdom comes from putting things together: *synthesis*.

John A. Morrison

Knowledge and wisdom, far from being one, have at times no connection.
Knowledge dwells in heads replete with thoughts of other men: wisdom in minds attentive to their own.
Knowledge is proud that she has learned so much.
Wisdom is humble that she knows no more.

Anonymous

Knowledge is power, but wisdom is liberty.

Will Durant

Nine-tenths of wisdom is being wise in time.

Theodore Roosevelt

The recipe for perpetual ignorance is: Be satisfied with your opinions and content with your knowledge.

Elbert Hubbard

Knowledge is only an instrument in the hands of wisdom.

Great minds discuss ideas and principles; mediocre minds discuss events, and the business at hand. Small minds discuss other people's business.

Quoted by Tom Morris

No man is so foolish but he may sometimes give another good counsel, and no man so wise that he may not easily err if he takes no other counsel than his own. He that is taught only by himself has a fool for a master.

Ben Jonson

There is always a frontier where there is an open mind and a willing hand.

Charles F. Kettering

Genius is:
- The power to visualize the objective
- Constancy of purpose
- The ability to make continuous effort.

Thomas S. Monson

If the power to do hard work is not talent, it is the best possible substitute for it.

James A. Garfield

Imagination decides everything.

Blaise Pascal

Nurture your mind with great thoughts: to believe in heroes makes heroes.

Benjamin Disraeli

That which we can conceive and believe, we can achieve.

Norman Vincent Peale

If a person has talent and somehow learns to use the whole of it, then that person has gloriously succeeded and has won a satisfaction and triumph few people shall ever know.

Thomas Wolfe

We are told that talent creates its own opportunities. We also find that *intense desire* creates not only its own opportunities, but its own *talents*.

Eric Hoffer

If you have built castles in the air, your work need not be lost: that is where they should be. Now go, and put foundations under them.

Henry David Thoreau

Genius is at first little more than a great capacity for receiving discipline.

George Eliot

Will is the measure of power. To a great genius there must be a great will. If the thought is not a lamp to the will, does not proceed to an act, the wise are imbecile. He alone is strong and happy who has a will. The rest are herds: he uses, they are used. He is the Maker; they are the made.

Ralph Waldo Emerson

No problem can be solved from the same consciousness that created it. We must learn to see the world anew.

Albert Einstein

Let us realize that the privilege to work is a gift, the power to work is a blessing, the love of work is success. Genius undoubtedly is little more than the capacity for hard, sustained work.

David O. McKay

It is difficult to say what is impossible, for the dream of yesterday is the hope of today and the reality of tomorrow.

Robert H. Goddard,
world's first rocket scientist

There are two kinds of failures: The man who will do nothing he is told, and the man who will do nothing else.

Perle Thompson

Your mind and a parachute are both useless if they remain closed.

Anonymous

The teacher sent home a note pinned to the 6-year-old boy. The note read: "This child is too stupid to learn." The boy's name? Thomas A. Edison.

MISCELLANEOUS /
UNCLASSIFIED

They are never alone who are accompanied with noble thoughts.

Philip Sydney

Strength does not come from physical capacity. It comes from an indomitable will.

Mahatma Gandhi

Whenever men are deeply stirred, whenever they are moved by grandeur or awed by mightiness of spirit, there is a God-given instinct to write down what they feel and see. And these become words to live by, whether they are the commandments engraved on a tablet of stone, or verses written on the back of a letter by the dawn's early light.

Thomas Dreier

An open mind, like an open window, should be screened to keep the bugs out.

Virginia Hutchinson

Peace cannot be kept by force. It can only be achieved by understanding.

Albert Einstein

Nothing is invented and perfected at the same time.

John Ray

The absurd man is he who never changes his opinion.

Auguste Bartolemy

Men are not against you; they are merely *for* themselves.

Gene Fowler

Try to give ten sincere compliments a day, to ten different people. You'll find that your whole world changes by the accomplishment of this one goal.

Anonymous

Whoever fears to submit any question to the test of free discussion loves his opinion more than he loves the truth.

Anonymous

Do, every day, something no one else would be silly enough to do.

Christopher Morley

When you're average, you're as close to the bottom as to the top.

Anonymous

Happy laughter and friendly voices in the home will keep more kids off the streets than the loudest curfew.

Burton Hillis

When a child gets what he wants, you can be sure he is well on the way toward delinquency.

Kenneth W. Lund

Every boy, in his heart, would rather steal second base than an automobile.

Anonymous

A switch, says the old railroader, has put many a delinquent on the right track.

Anonymous

For my soul delighteth in the song of the heart; yea, the song of the righteous is a prayer unto me, and it shall be answered with a blessing upon their heads.

Doctrine & Covenants 25:12

Wherefore, do not spend money for that which is of no worth, nor your labor for that which cannot satisfy.

2 Nephi 9:51

Honor thy father and thy mother.

Exodus 20:12

Cease to sleep longer than is needful; retire to thy bed early, that ye may not be weary; arise early, that your bodies and your minds may be invigorated.

Doctrine & Covenants 88:124

But lay up for yourselves treasures in heaven, where neither moth nor rust doth corrupt, and where thieves do not break through nor steal.

3 Nephi 13:20

And see that all these things are done in wisdom and order; for it is not requisite that a man should run faster than he has strength.

Mosiah 4:27

Smile well and often. It makes people wonder what you're up to.

Sachel Paige

It is advantageous to anyone to come to know the most universal principles with which he may govern his life.

Aristotle

Confidence-restoring activity: Make a list called THINGS I HAVE ACCOMPLISHED ALREADY.

All that is necessary for the triumph of evil is that good men do nothing.

Edmund Burke

It is not what people gain, but what they save, that makes them rich. It is not what they read, but what they remember and apply, that makes them learned.

Henry Ward Beecher

Not everybody is going to like you. In fact, some people are going to hate and detest you. And it's the very things that some like most about you that others will find the most repulsive. This is the human condition. You can't please everybody. Don't even try.

Anonymous

The formula for a good speech: have a good beginning, a great ending, and keep the two as close together as possible.

Anonymous

He who gossips to you will also gossip about you.

Anonymous

A man is rich in proportion to the number of things he can do without.

Henry David Thoreau

Blessed are the peacemakers: for they shall be called the children of God.

Matthew 5:9

If you would not be forgotten as soon as you are dead, either write things worth reading, or do things worth writing about.

Voltaire

Testimonies
Ask / Seek / Search

Ask, and it shall be given unto you; seek, and ye shall find; knock, and it shall be opened unto you.

3 Nephi 14:7

Every man has within himself a continent of undiscovered character. Happy is he who proves the Columbus of his soul.

Goethe

He who know others is clever, but he who knows himself is enlightened.

Lao Tse

To be conscious that you are ignorant is a great step to knowledge.

Benjamin Disraeli

If any of you lack wisdom, let him ask of God, that giveth to all men liberally, and upbraideth not; and it shall be given him.

James 1:5

But seek ye first the kingdom of God and his righteousness, and all these things shall be added unto you.

3 Nephi 13:33

From contemplation one may become wise, but knowledge comes only from study.

A. Edward Newton

Whosoever acquires knowledge, and did not practice it, resembleth him who ploughed and did not sow.

Saadi

Search these commandments, for they are true and faithful, and the prophecies and promises which are in them shall all be fulfilled.

Doctrine & Covenants 1:37

Feast upon the words of Christ; for behold, the words of Christ will tell you all things what ye should do.

2 Nephi 32:3

Seek ye out of the best books words of wisdom; seek learning, even by study and also by faith.

Doctrine & Covenants 88:118

For my soul delighteth in the scriptures, and my heart pondereth them, and writeth them for the learning and the profit of my children.

2 Nephi 4:15

Seek not for riches but for wisdom, and behold, the mysteries of God shall be unfolded unto you, and then shall you be made rich. Behold, he that hath eternal life is rich.

Doctrine & Covenants 6:7

Have ye spiritually been born of God? Have ye received his image in your countenances? Have ye experienced this mighty change in your hearts?

Alma 5:14

Search diligently, pray always, and be believing, and all things shall work together for your good.

Doctrine & Covenants 90:24

And blessed are all they who do hunger and thirst after righteousness, for they shall be filled with the Holy Ghost.

3 Nephi 12:6

Wisdom is the principal thing; therefore get wisdom; and with all thy getting get understanding.

Proverbs 4:7

I have found that the questions of life are far more important than the answers. We can be satisfied with different answers at different points in our life. But it is the questions which keep us searching and growing.

R. Dale Jeffery

And whatsoever ye shall ask the Father in my name, which is right, believing that ye shall receive, behold it shall be given unto you.

3 Nephi 18:20

Worship is an individual activity, even at church. If one wishes to worship the Lord, they may do so by song, prayer and participation in the sacrament. If the service is a failure, it is YOU who have failed. No one can worship for you.

Spencer W. Kimball

Vision / Goals / Goal-Setting

We make our own destiny . . . We can satisfy ourselves with mediocrity. We can be common, ordinary, dull, colorless, or we can so channel our lives to be clean, vibrant, progressive, colorful, and rich.

Spencer W. Kimball

Nurture your mind with great thoughts: to believe in heroes makes heroes.

Benjamin Disraeli

I find the great thing in this world is not so much where we stand as in what direction we are moving: To reach the port of Heaven, we must sail sometimes with the wind and sometimes against it—but we must sail, and not drift, nor lie at anchor.

Oliver Wendell Holmes

You can live the impossible dream, or you can live an excuse. It's all up to you.

Paul Kane

Don't bother just to be better than your contemporaries and predecessors; try to be better than yourself.

Charlie T. Jones

We shouldn't spend our lives solving little problems: we need to learn how to live with the little problems, and get on to bigger and better ones.

David M. Kennedy

To accomplish great things we must not only act, but also dream; not only plan, but also believe.

Anatole Frances

No life ever grows great until it is focused, dedicated and disciplined.

Henry Emerson Fosdick

Our lives are what our thoughts create.

Anonymous

You must have long-range goals to keep you from being frustrated by short-range failures.

Charles C. Noble

It is better to undertake a large task and get it half done than to undertake nothing and get it all done.

W. Marshall Craig

We may not achieve our ideals, but, like the stars, they serve to guide us on our way.

Anonymous

Some men see things as they are and say, "Why?" I dream things that never were, and say, "Why not?"

George Bernard Shaw

In the long run, people hit only what they are aiming at.   Therefore . . . they had better aim at something high.

Henry David Thoreau

You have powers you never dreamed of. You can do things you never thought you could do. There are no limitations in what you can do except the limitations as to what you cannot do. Don't think you cannot. Think that you can.

Darwin P. Kingsley

One of the most durable satisfactions in life is to lose one's self in one's work.

Henry Emerson Fosdick

The creation of a thousand forests is in one acorn.

Ralph Waldo Emerson

I cannot do great things by myself, but I can do small things in a great way.

James Freeman Clarke

Character is the ability to follow through with the objective or commitment long after the original motivation has passed.

Quoted by Larry Beckham

A goal is nothing more than a dream with a due date.

Joseph Fielding McConkie

A goal not written is only a wish.

Missionary Handbook

We do not suddenly become what we do not participate in becoming.

William H. Bennett

We can only know where we are in relation to where we want to be.

Paul H. Dunn

Those who can envision the most can accomplish the most.

Anonymous

Besides the noble art of getting things done, there is the noble art of leaving things undone. The wisdom of life consists in the elimination of non-essentials.

Lin Yu Tang

Edison once was asked how he accomplished so much. He said, "It is deceptively simple. You and I have eighteen hours in a day in which we do something. You spend that eighteen hours doing a number of unrelated things. I spend it doing just one thing, and some of my work is bound to amount to something."

Quoted by Sterling W. Sill

While we may surpass our goals, we can never surpass our dreams. The extent to which we can achieve is therefore only limited by the breadth of our vision and our capacity to follow through.

R. Dale Jeffery